HOW TO STAY SEXUALLY ATTRACTIVE IN MARRIAGE

Bryan Parker

Table of content

Introduction

The beginning of a relationship is frequently full of passion: thinking about each other continuously and wanting to spend every waking minute together – in and out of the bedroom. It's all-consuming.

But more often than not, that sort of intoxicating infatuation dissipates with time.

In long-term partnerships, it's fairly unusual for attraction between partners to diminish, we take for granted that just because we were attracted to our spouse once, the same attraction will persist forever without effort.

First thing someone observes about another individual is surely their looks and their appearance. Even in cases of love, the essential factor that draws a person to another is their masquerade and the way they seem. However, it is not the only aspect that appeals to the eyes of a man or woman. According to specialists, the most typical reason couples lose their desire for one other and cease being sexually intimate is a pursuer-distancer cycle that develops over time. It is one of three "Demon Dialogues." When one spouse becomes critical and confrontational, the other frequently becomes protective and aloof.

Partners who become locked in this cycle in the first few years of marriage have more than an 80 percent probability of divorcing in the first four to five years.

Chapter 1

Cultivate Emotional Intimacy

A successful sexual connection is founded on

emotional intimacy and closeness. In other words, if you're wanting to strengthen your physical relationship, you need to first concentrate on your emotional connection. Focus on satisfying your partner's needs and conveying your own wants in a loving, respectful manner.

In The Science of Trust, Dr. Gottman emphasizes that couples who wish to reignite their passion and love need to turn towards one another. Practicing emotional attunement may help you remain connected even when you disagree. This involves leaning toward one another through exhibiting empathy, instead than becoming defensive. Both spouses need to communicate about their sentiments in terms of positive need, instead of what they do not need.

Expressing a positive need is a formula for success for both the listener and the speaker since it transmits concerns and requests without judgment and blame. This involves a conceptual transition from what is wrong with one's spouse to what one's partner can do that would work. The speaker is essentially expressing, 'Here's what I feel, and what I need from you.

Rekindle Sexual Chemistry

Holding hands, embraces, and delicate contact are fantastic methods to reinforce your love for your mate. Physical affection sets the foundation for sexual contact that is focused on pleasure. Sex therapist and educator Dr. Micheal Stysma suggests that you set a goal of doubling the amount of time you kiss, embrace, and employ sensual contact if you want to enhance your marriage.

Sexual lulls are natural even for the most ardent couples — and they might really be a positive thing. One researcher attributed one element of the problem to ennui: the emotional sense of boredom is hard to ignore, and in this manner it indirectly helps individuals participate. The issue isn't the fact that passion fades, it's that we're so unprepared when it does. Hot sex is easy during the honeymoon period of a relationship and then things eventually start to cool down. The simple conclusion is that we're predisposed to desire surprise, variation, and adventure — while long-term relationships are the exact opposite. Stability is the enemy of the unexpected. Routine wipes away variety." Advice: Prioritize sex as much as any area of the relationship, and attempt to bring back the diversity and surprise.

Chapter 2

How to keep sexually appealing in marriage

1. Change your tendency of initiating sex

Maybe you are rejecting your lover or coming on too hard. Avoid criticizing one other and end the "blame game." Mix things up to stop the power struggle. For example, distancers may wish to practice initiating sex more frequently while pursuers attempt to discover methods to tell their partner "you're sexy," in subtle ways while avoiding judgement and requests for proximity.

2. Hold hands more frequently

According to author Dr. Kory Floyd, holding hands, embracing, and touching may produce oxytocin creating a relaxing effect. Studies suggest it's also produced during sexual climax. Additionally, physical love decreases stress hormones — reducing daily levels of the stress hormone cortisol.

3. Allow strain to develop

Our brains sense greater pleasure when the anticipation of the reward goes on for some time before we get it. So take your time during foreplay, exchange dreams, change venues, and make sex more romantic.

4. Separate sexual intimacy from routine
Plan intimate time and avoid talking about marital troubles and domestic duties in the bedroom. Sexual arousal plummets when we're preoccupied and worried.
5. Carve out time to spend with your spouse
Try a range of hobbies that provide you both pleasure. Have fun courting and practice flirting as a technique to generate sexual desire and connection.
6. Focus on loving touch
Offer to give your lover a back or shoulder massage. People equate foreplay with sexual intercourse, yet friendly contact is a strong technique to display and reignite desire even if you are not a touchy-feely type.
7. Practice becoming more emotionally vulnerable during sex
Share your deepest aspirations, fantasies, and wants with your spouse. If you dread emotional closeness, try

enrolling in solo or couple's counseling.

8. Maintain a feeling of curiosity about sexual intimacy

Experiment with novel techniques to provide pleasure to each other. Look at sex as a chance to get to know your spouse better over time.

9. Vary the sort of sex you have

Have gentle, loving-tender, intimate, and very passionate sex. Break up the pattern and explore new things when sexual needs vary.

10. Make sex a priority

Set the environment for intimacy before TV or job dulls your desire. A small lunch paired with your favorite music and wine may set the atmosphere for excellent sex.

Chapter 3

Ways to Refresh Your Marriage

Sometimes it's tough to comprehend your partner. Let's be honest, we communicate and think differently than our other half. To keep your marital connection fresh and developing stronger, each partner must practice being sensitive to the other person's wants and desires. When a husband and wife effectively merge their two viewpoints, harmony and understanding is established in the marriage. Whether your marriage is hurting or you simply want to mix things up a little, here are some suggestions for establishing togetherness and gaining a grasp on bliss:

1. **Be romantic**.

Great romance doesn't simply happen, it's planned. Place priority on seeking out fresh methods to convey "I love you." Husbands, take the time to be romantic and your wife will be a more passionate lover. Wife, convey your opinions about how you wish to be romanced. Don't make him guess!

2. Compliment each other.
Decide to commend your spouse on at least one item every day. Be cautious to listen. Your partner will complement you on areas in which he/she desires to receive
compliments. Be careful to avoid from back-handed compliments.
3. Date your spouse.
Don't lose the lovin' sensation you had when you first began dating. Commit to frequent, planned date evenings, and take turns picking the agenda. Don't accept calls or messages throughout your date. Refrain from discussing about difficult things such as money, kids, or job. This is the moment to revive hopes and new concepts for the future.
4. Share your time.
This is your life, right now. Don't become so busy that you forget to calm down and appreciate life—and to enjoy it with your spouse. It's a compliment when your partner wants to spend time

with you. Plan out and prioritize your schedule. Designate time for resting, going out, and performing tasks.

5. Be spontaneous.

Do something out of the norm for your spouse once a week. Sometimes you need to plan ahead, yet do something to surprise your spouse, something they would never expect you to do. Stretching yourself and your partner may be a great developing experience! Draw closer to one another in the midst of the unknown.

6. Make communication a priority.

Learn your mate's communication style. Everyone communicates differently. Tell him or her the greatest method to talk with you. Pay attention and actively listen to what your spouse has to say: nod, react, and make eye contact.

7. Listen.

Devote your complete attention to what your spouse is saying rather than utilizing the opportunity to plan your own answer. Restate your spouse's comments, repeating what they said, and then carefully answer. Discern what role your husband wants you to play in a discussion, whether as a passive listener or an active issue solver and opinion provider.

8. Sex—take your job seriously.

Great sex is the duty of both partners. Be desired. Work with what you have and present yourself as appealing as possible. Seek to meet your spouse's needs before your own. And don't be hesitant to schedule sex. You may become enthusiastic about your plan and look forward to your time together.

9. Support change.

You and your spouse will change throughout the course of your marriage and it's crucial to embrace those changes. Continue to appreciate and trust each other, but don't attempt to hold the other back from growth—it's easy for resentment to sleep in when you do. If you need additional assistance, ask!

10. Serve your spouse.

If you are both putting the other first, your needs will never go unsatisfied. Start serving now! Make the initial move and watch as your partner reciprocates. Never cease complimenting your spouse for even the apparently banal things.

11. Celebrate milestones.

Be deliberate about building memories with your partner, particularly during holidays, birthdays, anniversaries, etc. Create your own events and customs as a pair. If a day is extremely meaningful to one partner, commemorate it the way he or she wants to. Make sure both of you have fun during vacations!

12. Apologize and forgive.

Be the first one to say "I'm sorry." Take your pain to God and let go of whatever anger, animosity, or power you have over your companion. Are you carrying a grudge? Tell your spouse you forgive them. Do you need to beg for forgiveness? Do it today. Take Paul's words to heart: "do not let the sun go set on your wrath" (Ephesians 4:26).

13. Balance independence and reliance.

Sometimes you need distance, and sometimes you need greater closeness. Tell your partner what you need, when you need it. Wives, recognize his intrinsic need to be independent—encourage him in activities that meet that urge. Husbands, know that she wants to be your partner—include her in decision making.

14. Put your spouse's needs above your own.

Think of how your marriage might alter if you and your spouse both implemented this scripture; "Let nothing be done from selfish ambition or conceit, but in lowliness of mind let everyone regard others better than himself. Let everyone watch out not only for his own interests, but also for the interests of others." Philippians 2:3-4

15. In all these things, seek the Lord first.
Husbands and wives, pursue a growing relationship with the Lord. As we grow and evolve as people, so will our marriages. But these changes may make us stronger if we consistently seek the Lord and His knowledge, because "...He is a rewarder of those who earnestly seek Him" (Hebrews 11:6).

Chapter 4

Sexercise to keep you sexually fit in marriage
You know that exercising out is important for your health. But did you know that going the gym might also help you have better sex? Working out three to four times a week can do a lot to help your sexual technique, flexibility, and endurance.
Stamina can mean many things, but when it comes to sex, it often refers to how long you can last in bed.

For guys, the typical duration between the sheets is anything from two to five minutes. For females, it's a little longer: roughly 20 minutes before hitting the big O.

If you're frustrated with how fast you do the deed, there are a number of things you may do to raise your endurance and improve your overall sexual performance

Healthy methods to enhance Sexual Stamina: Tips to Improve Strength and Endurance.

So what sorts of exercise are ideal for better sex?

Pelvic floor

Your pelvic floor regulates your genitals, which means if you want to boost your sexual stamina, you need to grow strong — and flexible — pelvic floor muscles.

Exercises to attempt include:

Kegels

Squats

bridges

Glutes

Weak glutes can throw off your balance and stiffen your

hips, which will affect your performance in bed.

Exercises to attempt include:

squats

weighted lunges

hip extension

Quads and hamstrings

Your quad and hamstrings power your hips and knees, which means the stronger those muscles are, the quicker and longer you can run.

Exercises to attempt include:

leg press

lunges

Biceps

Stronger biceps implies you can manage more weight while lifting, pulling, tossing, and throwing.

Exercises to attempt include:

Bicep curls

chin-ups

bent-over row

Triceps

Strong triceps not only make pushing simpler, but they also build up the power of your upper body.

Exercises to attempt include:

bench press

triceps extension

triceps pull-down or push-down

Pectoral

You utilize your pectoral muscles for everything you do - from opening a door to raising a drink. When you have stronger pecs, you have a stronger physique overall.

Exercises to attempt include:

Bench press
chest dips
push-ups

Abdominal

When you have strong abs, you have a more powerful core. And when you have a strong core, you're more balanced and suffer less back discomfort.

Exercises to attempt include:

sit-ups
planks
high knees

Lower back

A strong lower back stabilizes and supports your spine, as well as helping strengthen your core.

Exercises to attempt include:

bridges
lying lateral leg raise
superman extension

Tongue strengthening
When it comes to sex, the great book She Comes First says that the vagina-carrying population experiences orgasm by cunnilingus 81 percent of the time, compared with 25 percent of the time with vaginal intercourse. Therefore, it behooves those of us who like fulfilling such persons to learn expertise with oral sex.
One crucial prerequisite is tongue endurance – you need to be able to linger long enough to fire your partner up! Fortunately, you can strengthen your tongue.
Strengthening your tongue may also aid enhance your breathing, as well as boost your endurance for oral sex.
Exercise to attempt include:
Tongue pull-back.
Stick your tongue out straight, then drag it back in your mouth as far as you can. Hold this posture for 2 seconds. Repeat 5 times.
Tongue push-ups.
Push the bottom of the tip of your tongue as firmly as you

can onto the front of the roof of your mouth, exactly behind your teeth. Repeat 5 to 10 times.

Chapter 5

Foods That Increase Your Sexual Stamina and Sex Drive

Having a good sex drive is connected to feeling physically and emotionally well. So it's no surprise that food may play a part in helping you get your rhythm back. If you've reached a downturn in the bedroom, it may be time to take a closer look at your food. These eleven meals are rich with nutrients that help liven up your libido and may benefit your general health, too. Any nutritious meal is helpful for sex. However, there are some products that are especially useful

1) Watermelon:

Watermelon is one of the finest natural sources of L-citrulline, a non-essential amino acid that your body converts to L-arginine in your body. And it's the L-arginine that might help make your erection harder. Like the tiny blue tablet, L-arginine promotes the creation of nitric oxide, which increases blood flow to the penis, increasing erections.

2) Apples:

An apple a day doesn't simply keep the doctor away; it may also aid to lengthen your sexual stamina. It's all down to apples' high amounts of quercetin, an antioxidant flavonoid that has been discovered to have a role in increasing endurance. And because your body goes through many of the same physical changes during sex that it does during exercise—elevated heart rate, higher metabolism, expended calories, and muscular contractions—you might equate endurance with prolonging your time in bed.

3) Ginger:

Ginger is another food that may increase your sex life by

helping blood flow and enhancing arterial health. According to a research in the International Journal, ingesting a mere spoonful of the substance a few times a week is all you need to gain the heart-healthy advantages. So, go ahead and place that second order of sushi this week—just don't leave the ginger on your plate.

4) Bananas:

Banana fruit is rich of simple carbohydrates to supply you with energy and potassium to help you stay going. The muscle-relaxing mineral reduces cramps and muscular spasms that may impair your sexy time. Plus, the American Heart Association states that potassium may help reduce blood pressure, which can increase sexual performance by assuring normal blood flow to various regions of the body, including the genitals.

5) Garlic:

According to historians, ancient Egyptians utilized garlic to enhance their stamina. A Journal of

Nutrition research demonstrated that ingesting garlic extract may help reduce the creation of new fatty deposits, termed plaque, within artery walls. Yes, it includes the arteries going to your penis, too. Keep your heart healthy and your erections robust by adding some garlic to your weekly dinners.

6) Pomegranate Juice:

A recent research published in the International Journal of Impotence Research revealed that pomegranate juice, rich in antioxidants that enhance blood flow, may help alleviate erectile dysfunction. Though this research was supported by POM Wonderful, animal studies have also indicated that the elixir increases long-term erectile responsiveness.

7) Beets:

It helps enhance general blood flow—which is also excellent for your thinking. In a recent Physiology & Behavior research, adult volunteers were given a dosage of beet juice and then conducted a variety of cognitive tests. The researchers observed that the beet juice dramatically boosted blood flow to their brains and enhanced cognitive ability. The hidden power of these roots? Nitrates, which are contained in beets are turned into nitrite in the body & consequently enhances Sexual Power.

8) Avocado:

A shortage of B-vitamins—nutrients that keep nerves and brain cells healthy—could possibly be aggravating your stress even more, finds a Nutrition Journal research. The solution? Not only are avocados rich in stress-relieving B vitamins, but they're also a source of monounsaturated fat, which has been found to assist blood flow to the whole body—including the penis

9) Meat:

Include a variety of meats in your diet to boost your sex life. Beef, chicken, and pork contain carnitine, L-arginine, and zinc. Carnitine and L-arginine are amino acids that improve blood flow. Uninterrupted blood flow is crucial to sexual response in both men and women. According to NYU Langone Medical Center, these two nutrients may effectively treat erectile dysfunction in some men.

10) Oysters:

You've probably heard about the aphrodisiac properties of oysters. Research shared at a 2005 conference of the American Chemical Society that oysters, clams, and scallops contain compounds that raise testosterone and estrogen levels. A boost in hormone production translates into heightened sexual desire in many cases. Oysters are also an excellent source of zinc, which aids blood flow to sexual organs in both genders.

11)Eggs:

Consume eggs for a healthy erection. Eggs contain amino acid L-arginine that can improve erectile dysfunction. While certain foods can keep your blood pumping and boost hormone levels, diet alone isn't always enough to improve your sex life. Speak to your doctor if a lack of desire, pain during intercourse, or impotence is holding you back from enjoying an intimate relationship with your partner.

Conclusion

Why Sex Is Important

Can a relationship survive without sex? Why Sex Is Important

Yes. Sex isn't always essential. But it may be a crucial aspect of a good, successful relationship.

How vital sex is may differ from one person to the next. Some individuals may believe that having a sexual relationship is extremely necessary. Others may believe that other sorts of closeness and connection are more vital.

Some of the reasons why you may believe that sex is vital in a relationship include:
Feeling closer to your lover.
Showing affection to your partner.
Finding sex fun and pleasurable.
A desire to have children.
Feeling confident and sexy.
Relieving tension.
Research shows that having regular sex might have a role in a person's general well-being. Having sex frequently is connected to increased affection. When partners feel greater affection, they are also more likely to later have more frequent intercourse.
Sex may be a vital component of a relationship but having sex less regularly does not always indicate that your relationship is any less pleasant.

www.ingramcontent.com/pod-product-compliance
Lightning Source LLC
LaVergne TN
LVHW020543160826
845677LV00015B/4179

9798352575437